A SIMPLE STONE

Raymond

2007

A Simple Stone

Raymond F. Bergeron

Published by Alabaster Book Publishing
North Carolina

This is a work of fiction. Names, characters, places, and incidents either are the product of the author's imagination or are used fictitiously and any resemblance to actual persons, businesses, events, or locales is coincidental.

Copyright 2007 by Raymond F. Bergeron
All rights reserved. Printed in the United States of America. No part of this book may be reproduced in any manner whatsoever without written permission except in the case of brief quotations embodied in critical articles and reviews.

Published by Alabaster Books
P.O. Box 401
Kernersville, North Carolina 27285
www.publisheralabaster.biz

Book and cover design by
D.L.Shaffer
Cover Photo by Rich Warner

First Edition

ISBN:978-0-9790949-5-8

Library of Congress Control Number
2007901631

This book of poems is dedicated to my "little bride",
Sharon.

My wife, your love I need.
You listen to me read
The words I've freed.

You type my misspelled words,
Some I never heard.

Your computer skills
The disk you fill.

My words to store
So I can write more.

Thank you Mrs. B.
To type all the words I see.

I love thee!

ACKNOWLEDGEMENTS

My poetry began with a dream. I saw a spirit rise out of a grave. She wanted me to write a poem about her tombstone. I explained that I wasn't a writer. She said she would help me and she gave me five words:

A simple stone, birth, death

From these words I wrote the first of many poems:

A simple stone
carved by flesh and bone.
A birth!
A breath!
A death!
What wrath!
This path
I walk alone
to sit a hearth
not my own.

So I thank my "Muse" who has released my inner thoughts.

I also want to thank Rich Warner for the photograph of the cover of the book; Allan Swenson for his encouragement to publish this book; Rev. E. Lamar Robinson for his friendship and spiritual guidance; my three kids and their spouses: Jayne and Fred, Michael and Lisa, and Mark and Beckie for their support.

CONTENTS

Poems Concerning

Nature	1
Raymond	37
Family	49
Friends	59
Christ	97
Faith	117
Humanity	129

A Simple Stone

Nature

Raymond F. Bergeron

A Simple Stone

SIMPLE STONE

A simple stone
Carved by flesh and bone.

A birth!
A breath!
A death!

What wrath,
This path

I walk alone
To sit a hearth

Not my own.

A poem request
From spirits turbulent rest
Locked by this rock.

A tombstone quest
Of birth and death.

Spirit seek
My soul to find.

Raymond F. Bergeron

From the darkness
Of my mind.

Sleep secret plight
In the silent night.

Thank you!
Spirit free.

My mind caressed,
My words unleashed.

Rest in peace
With God to feast.

A Simple Stone

STONE WALL

Ten thousand years ago
From ice and snow,
Glaciers began to grow.

Their huge masses
gorged through mountain passes.

Its rock to grind
today, you still find.

Across this land
beautiful stonewalls still stand.

Built!
By the hand of man.

They bent their backs
these stones to stack.

To feel the pain
as they strained
on more stone to gain.

Father and Son
From dawn to setting sun.

Raymond F. Bergeron

Stone by stone they begun
until their work was done.

Built to stay!
Some go straight-a-way,
Boundaries to this day.

Some ramble through fields and wood.
The test of time they stood.

A place for snakes to roam
in moss covered, gray stones.
Chipmunks make their homes.

With simple stones
these walls stand alone.

Built
by flesh and bone.

By Father and Son
Raymond F. and Mark R. Bergeron

A Simple Stone

WINTER'S END

Life
From death.

Vulture in the sky
Winter soon to die.

This bird,
This death seeker.

It feels winter's pulse
Growing weaker.

This black gloom
Its bones to consume.

The spring has won.
Winter's tomb begun.

To the victor
Goes the spoils.

New life
From the soil.

Raymond F. Bergeron

WHIPPOORWILL

O' bird of night
Your heart sings a new song.

You coo like the morning dove,
A song of love.

Remember from where you flew,
From the darkness to the light.

Beware the rapture,
Of a breaking dawn.

It may blind your sight,
O' bird of night.

A Simple Stone

MOCKING BIRD

Hark the mocking bird,
Awake my midnights slumber.

Piping your magic flute,
Your melodies echoing the morning mist.

Mimic the meadowlark,
And chase away my dark.

Your singing dawns my light,
From the jet of night.

Sleep, my barless cage,
Where the cryptic horrors rage.

A dungeon of demonic dreams,
That devours my unconscious.

I cannot escape their nocturnal embrace,
I tremble, with fear that shackles my soul.

Awake my dormant ears,
To hear the chorus that quells my quaking.

Raymond F. Bergeron

BUTTERFLY

To be a butterfly
A caterpillar must change.

A lowly larval slug
A greedy little bug.

They gorge their gut
To eat and excrete.

Mass quantities to consume,
To make their own tomb.

In time pupa must change.
To cast off old ways.

To embrace a new day
A metamorphic struggle

To free the shackles of the past.

A new life to begin
To dance on the wind.

Oh! To be a butterfly
You must change.

A Simple Stone

CRESCENT MOON

Rise,
Oh crescent moon.

Your slender silhouette
Carves the evening jet.

A silver slit in seamless sky.
A single night of shadowed sphere.

To slide below horizon's door
And return once more.

To rise,
Larger than before.

Raymond F. Bergeron

A ROSE

A rose.
It's beauty lost.

The thorn of death
Pierced its heart.

This bud of life
Its bloom consumed.

Withered on the stem
Never to grow again.

A Simple Stone

DANDELION I

Dandelion
King of weeds, gone to seed.

Dethroned, by the wind
Its golden mane shed.

Turned to fluff.
Gone in a single puff.

Unseen below the turf
The lion's heart beats.

Its roots thrust the earth.
Home of its birth.

New life begun
Once more to roar in the sun.

Raymond F. Bergeron

DANDELION II

Dandelion greens,
A gourmet's dream.

A bitter delight
Some don't like.

Just wash and steam
This weedy green.

With vinegar and salt pork fried crisp,
Boiled red bliss and cod fish.

Grandma's favorite dish.

A Simple Stone

RESTING PLACE

Man and Wife
In life and death.

Mary and John Hovey
Lay abreast.

By tide and marsh hay
They rest.

In family plot
That time forgot.

A wall of stones
Guards their earthly home.

One square rod
Of hallowed sod.

By the sea
Wed for eternity.

Raymond F. Bergeron

FIRST SNOW

Full moon glow

On virgin snow.

Sparkling bright

Like a diamond in the light.

Trees, dark sentinels of the night,

Forest secrets keep,

Their silent midnight shadows creep.

A mystical moment to behold

To live forever in my soul.

A Simple Stone

I CUT DOWN A TREE

I cut down a tree
for firewood need.

I count the rings
to know how old it be.

Years! The same as me.
Now ash, stump, and brush.

Will we meet again
when I am dust?

To grow anew
a tree I once slew.

Raymond F. Bergeron

ICE STORM

Winter storm
Of ice and snow.
The trees encased
With a frozen embrace.
The beauty of frosted snow
Clings to all things
Like a giant wedding cake
Mother Nature just baked.
Birch trees bow to the Earth,
Their roots they search.
Pines with broken crowns
Litter the ground.
No more to reach the sky,
Lie here to die.
Maple split in half.
A mighty stroke to snap.
In spring!
No sap, to tap.
Old man winter
Won this round.
I long to see
Bare ground.
When spring flowers
Can be found.
Birds to nest
And sing a song.

A Simple Stone

Maine winters
Are too damn long!

Raymond F. Bergeron

LEAVES

Leaves no longer thirst
The summer rain.

Their brilliant hues
In sunlight flash.

Earthward bound
The breezes cast.

To kiss their mother's cheek
And drink the autumn dew.

A Simple Stone

OLD RED BARN

Old red barn
On abandoned farm.

Built!
In a different way and day.

From the past
Its shadows cast.

From history we learned
When life slowly turned.

Things were made strong
To last long.

Forgotten!
Some ways are lost.
Oh! What a cost.

Our memories fade
From past days.

Who will show
What our forebearers used to know?

Raymond F. Bergeron

Don't abandon the past
So you can live fast.

Slow down
And look around, up and down.

You might like what you see.
Birds and flowers, or a tree.

Maybe!
This old red barn
On abandoned farm.

Things!
Like they used to be.

A Simple Stone

MAINE TO CALIFORNIA

From Maine's rocky shore
I hope to walk once more.
My wife and I journey west,
A new life to quest.

This odyssey from sea to shining sea.
While some question our sanity.
This land we girth
One-eighth of the Earth.

Our future in cardboard boxes packed,
The U-Haul to the roof is stacked.
We don't look back!

PA "Burgs", some we never heard.
Poconos and road kill,
The miles they fill.

Truckers southern drawl
And Cajun call.
Voices of America
In truck stop havens
They chatter like ravens.

Diesel fuel, coffee black
And pancakes by the stack.
Meatloaf and chicken fried steak,
Ain't it great!

Raymond F. Bergeron

Cowboy hats and pointed boots,
In their Macks and Peterbilts.
Down their routes they shoot.
In morning dawn, their diesel rush,
Beyond the evening dusk.

Great scenery this Virginia greenery.
Fog on a Tennessee Mountain top.
And a "Ville" over every hill.

5:42 A.M. in one minute we zip
Over the mighty Mississipp.
Flood plains, no crops they yield
Water standing in the fields.

Arkansas, what can I say,
There will be a new president someday.
This man from Hope
Didn't get my vote.

Texas rolls on and on.
From dawn to dusk and beyond.
From Texarkana to El Paso
We spend mucho Dinero.

"Construction straight ahead"
These words we dread.
"Right lane closed", "Merge left"
Our patience to test.
Will it end over the next crest?

Motels we quest
Our weary bones to rest.

A Simple Stone

In Pine Grove, PA
A buxom blonde we pay.
A farmer's daughter I'd say.

Greenville, Tennessee
Not the coal miner's daughter,
But Grandma, with chiseled jaw
Y'all – come – back – now.

A Memphis belle, this clerk from Hell.
Big, black and brash.
But she took our cash.

Ranger, Texas
She welcomed us with ivory grin
Hi-Ho she took our silver.
A Native American, a beauty
With raven hair and copper skin.

El Paso, Texas
A man of Spanish descent
Bargained for my last cent.

In Denny's Restaurant before the sun's arrival,
Christ and coffee with a preacher of revival.
From the Bible he did quote.
And I shared a verse I wrote.
These are the faces of America.

New Mexico,
Millions of yucca in bloom.
A carpet of white beyond our sight.

Raymond F. Bergeron

Arizona,
More of the same, how far we came.
To Casa Grande to visit Michael our son.
Dust devils swirl like another world.
Vultures on thermal rise,
And search their carrion prize.

California,
From below sea level,
We rise through mountain pass.
Hear the radiator gasp.
It thirsts, and so do we.
We make the grade
But find no shade.

Turn right at San Diego
On our left Pacific breakers crest.
We near our journey's quest.
Now we ride on the 405
Six lanes wide!

Finally reached
With family hugs and kisses greet.
Welcome to Long Beach!!!

A Simple Stone

BARSTOW BLUES

Desert's sights and sounds,
Freight train…Barstow bound.

From Barstow station,
Trains traverse the nation.

Hear their diesels sing,
Where echoes of the past still ring.

When steam was king,
And train bells went ding, ding, ding.

Engines had fires to stoke,
And belched black smoke.

With whistles that wailed,
Steeds of steel galloped on iron rails.

On high desert bluffs where the mountains thrust,
They bulge and billow from earth's crust.

Their brown and khaki hues,
Rupture the azure blue.

Where eagles and vultures fly,
And search their carrion prize.

Raymond F. Bergeron

Where sage brush and cacti,
Sound a sad good-bye.

A Simple Stone

IRON HORSES

Iron horses whinnying in the predawn,
Steel stallions, singing their sunrise song.

Diesels drone through the desert dust,
Hear their mighty engines thrust.

Hear their wishful whistles wail,
Homeward bound on silver rails.

Roaming over hill and vale,
Traversing their endless trail.

Awaken from my midnight slumber,
To hear their awesome gallop thunder.

Raymond F. Bergeron

RED TAIL HAWK

From perilous perch
she leaps to soar and search.
In lofty air
with eyes that stare.
Hear her cry
From upon high.
A fearful shriek,
Her talons seek their prey.
Nature's way she keeps.

A Simple Stone

SAILBOAT

Sailboat
Cradled and caged
From winter's rage.

Winter wraps shroud its grace
To hide its face
From north winds race.

Landlocked,
Beside the dock.

In cradle of steel
No sea to feel
Beneath its keel.

Earth bound
On frozen ground.

Spring tides rip
At winter's grip.

As seasons merge
Its ice to purge.

Raymond F. Bergeron

Awake!
From winter's rest.

New spring dress
Its hull caress.

From earthy way
It slides on tide
The wind to ride

Free!
On the sea.

A Simple Stone

SILENT SENTINEL

Silent sentinel
Stand erect.

Save from savage sea
Our ship to wreck.

To heave upon the rocky shore
And sail no more.

From mast's perilous perch
Your light we search.

Save from sea's violent surge
Our lives to purge.

Your beacon seek,
Our souls to keep.

Guide fiery spark
To harbors mark.

Raymond F. Bergeron

WOODPILE

Woodpile, weathered and cracked,
The cords neatly stacked.

Oak, Maple, and Beech.
The stove to feast,
When snow comes Nor'east.

To warm hearth and home,
When winter storms rage and roam.

Wood box fill,
Devour winter's chill.

Wood consumed.
Belch winter's doom.

Woodpile, weathered and cracked,
The cords neatly stacked.

A Simple Stone

CIRCLE OF LIFE

Milkweed pods and goldenrod.
Hydrangea in full bloom.

The fall they call
Summer on the wane.

Flowers beauty lost
To first frost.

Leaves on the trees their colors burst
Like a kaleidoscope.

Acorns, squirrels hope
For winter feast.

When the snow comes
Northeast.

Song birds flock
They hear the tick of nature's clock.

Geese to fly in a vee
For all to see.

Raymond F. Bergeron

Life will be too harsh
By frozen pond and marsh.

To the south they know to go.
From the ice and snow.

Mother Nature's show and tell
Her creatures learned well.

When the wind blows from the west
They like it best.

Wind from the north to blow,
It's time to go.

No calendar on the wall to know
For tiny seed to grow.

Sunrise in the east
Brings the spring.

Rebirth for the earth,
No beginning and no end.

In a spin to go again
Nature's quest goes round and round.

New life
Always to be found.

A Simple Stone

RAYMOND

Raymond F. Bergeron

A Simple Stone

GENERATIONS

I've pulled the Norseman's oar,
And sailed the newfound shore.

I've leaned on shepherd's crook,
Beside the alpine pasture brook.

I've fell the English Oak
That spans the castle moat.

I've worn a feathered crest
And beads upon my chest.

I've fished the cod
And praised one God!

I've plowed the furrow
Straight and deep.

The generations of the past
Long shadows cast.

I am a kaleidoscope
Of all their fears and hopes.

The blood has mingled
The generations…keep

Raymond F. Bergeron

RAYMOND

Raymond,
My Christian name
To life I came.

From my mother's womb,
My April breath,
Taurus true until death.

Mother Earth
Home, of my birthstone,
Never shone.

Diamond sleep
In the earth so deep.
Its light to keep.

My life to search
This fiery spark
To light my dark.

Diamond bright
This gift of light
I write.

A Simple Stone

The darkness flees
The world to see
These words inside of me.

Raymond F. Bergeron

SELF DISCOVERY

A simple stone
Never shone

A chunk of rock
A few cuts unlock

To refine,
The light to shine

Is a diamond fair
Hidden there?

New life to share
Was it always there

For all to see
Except for me?

A Simple Stone

DIAMOND

Symbol of love and birth
Captured from the earth.

A precious gift
Our hearts to uplift.

All, are not gemstones
From earthy home.

To wear on finger fair
The light to search
From golden perch.

Or, on king's crown
to be found.

Some are just chips
The steel of life to grind
Our lives to refine.

Life's diamond dust
The wind, to blow away.

Dust to dust
In God to trust.

Raymond F. Bergeron

From it, He made us!

A Simple Stone

LOST IN THE DARKNESS

Lost in the darkness of my mind
New words I find
The light to shine.

The words roll from my pen
To give to my friends.

The more I give
This gift of light
The more my sight.

The light grows brighter
From the one who said,
"I'm no writer."

Is this gift
For new souls, to uplift?

Raymond F. Bergeron

MY KEEPER

I thank my Lord my God,
Saved from the reaper's sword.

My savior, shields my life and soul,
As robbers bold, steal my merchants gold.

With weapons of fear and death,
That can vanquish my mortal breath.

Yesterday becomes history,
And I search beyond the horizon.

The dawning of a new day,
And I will go where He leadeth me.

My destiny, the die is cast,
And I journey His new path.

A Simple Stone

HOSANNA SING!

A poem request
My Sunday best.

Before God and man
His praises to recite.

My voice,
My thoughts,
My Maine twang,
The words they rang.

Bold and strong!
Clear, for all to hear.

Faces of the church
My words to search.

Like church bells, my words tolled
Maybe, to touch their souls.

Raymond F. Bergeron

OLD DOG

I'm an old dog,
Running with the wolves of technology.

I'm an old dog, my fangs are worn,
And I'm weary from the battles and wounds of yesteryear.

The wolves, are a vicious pack,
They strip away your flesh,
And leave the bones for the vultures to consume.
No evidence that you once passed by here.

I'm an old dog,
Who will defend the past and fight for the future.

I'm an old dog,
But I can, and will learn new tricks!

A Simple Stone

FAMILY

Raymond F. Bergeron

A Simple Stone

GRAMMY HAWKINS

Some people
are like stars.
Their light still shines
long after their fire
has gone out.

Raymond F. Bergeron

BABY SISTER

June of '44
No father to hold or adore
Fighting for freedom on far away shore.

Big Brother, was the mister,
Who held and loved his baby sister.

New life,
In the time of strife.

New breath,
In a world of war and death.

Siblings three,
Now bud on family tree.

New hope for things yet to be,
To bloom beyond our destiny.

We have journeyed through history,
Carried by our memories.

Brother and Sisters,
A kaleidoscope of kin,
The bond of blood that flows within.

Love,

Big Brother

A Simple Stone

SHARON

She's just a country girl
With silver curls.

She wears diamonds and pearls
And all the treasures of the world.

But it's her kisses that set my heart a twirl,
'Cause she's just a country girl.

In silver and gold, she looks so bold,
But it's her hand I love to hold.

The bottom line, she's so fine,
'Cause she's just a country girl... My Valentine.

Raymond F. Bergeron

WIFE

My wife, your love I need.
You listen to me read
The words I've freed.

You type my misspelled words,
Some I never heard.

Your computer skills
The disk you fill.

My words to store
So I can write more.

Thank you Mrs. B.
To type all the words I see.

I love thee!

A Simple Stone

JAYNE ELIZABETH

Jayne Elizabeth
Your spring birth
New life on Earth.
What love a baby brings,
You made my heart sing.
In my hands to hold
I watched you grow
To be very bold.
Now thirty-one
With husband and two sons.
Your life to invest
In your family's quest.
My heart still sings
As I write this verse.
For you are my first
And only daughter.
I send to you, a big hug
From me and your mother.
For us there's no other.
Jayne Elizabeth
From first breath
To this day,
Proud to say
I'm your Dad.

Happy Birthday!
Love,
Dad

Raymond F. Bergeron

WEDDING VOWS

I do.
Simple words spoken from the heart,
Let no one part.

Before God and man be true,
I love you.

Wedded bliss,
Vows sealed with a tender kiss.

Passion's promises encircled by gold
May your love forever unfold.

Your souls,
Embraced beyond Eternity.

I am love!
I lift my cup to thee.

Michael and Lisa
September 28, 1996

Love DAD!

A Simple Stone

GENA

When I married your mother
You were already there.

Two girls with golden hair,
My heart to share.

Gena, a golden nugget, bright, beautiful and bold,
In my heart to forever hold.

Daddy's little girl with golden curls,
What gift will complete your world?

What precious gift can I impart,
To this little girl, grafted to my heart?

Like your sister Kayla, you both from heaven came,
I give you my name.

Written for my son Michael and his family to celebrate his daughter's official adoption, November 1998.

Raymond F. Bergeron

November 13, 2004

Eric,

    You are a first-born son! You come from a long line of first-born sons. Your Dad and his Grandfather are first-born. I myself, and my Dad and Grandfather are also first-born sons.

    Much is expected from our first-born sons: to stand straighter and reach beyond the horizon. You have already proven that you have the strength and faith to overcome life's pitfalls.

You come from strong blood, so hold your birthright banner high. With heritage and faith, march into the future.

With love,

Your proud Grampa!

PS: See Generations

A Simple Stone

FRIENDS

Raymond F. Bergeron

A Simple Stone

ODE TO MISS DWELLEY

Miss Dwelley,
my high school English teacher
and home room keeper.

After last bell I stayed
so I could make her grade.

My private hell, new words to spell
and to learn their meaning.

Some days,
I just stared at the ceiling.

A lady, very nice.
In the classroom she turned to ice.

Her rules she held firm,
Like the grip of a vise.

Break her rules
and you would pay the price.

I did.
My junior year to repeat.

Raymond F. Bergeron

Double trouble, in the same seat.
"All work must be complete
and on time!"

To fail is no crime.
Her class you would pass
only, if you tried.

To do your best
was her request.

Her time, in you she would invest
only, if you tried.

Yourself to test
to do your best.

I must confess
sometimes I fail this quest
to do my best.

To this day
I can hear say,
"Please, try again."

Class of '55 & "'56"

A Simple Stone

LADY WARRIOR

Lady warrior
No Amazon in leather thongs

The sword of strength and courage
Carried in gingham sheath.

The truth of life to seek
Your enemies to defeat.

Frail, but not meek.
To fight with no retreat.

Your tigress heart beats
The breath to keep.

In battle to defend,
To win again, and again.

Your spirit free
Ride on in victory!

Written for Amy Robinson, a young woman fighting a terminal illness.

Raymond F. Bergeron

WHIRLPOOL!

Whirlpool!

Earth quenching its thirst,
Engulfing all who sink

Into the center of nothingness,
From life's stress.

This spiral flood
To drain life's blood.

God hears your cry,
Your mortal plea.

From this whirling sea,
Your faith in Him

Will set you free.

Written For Elaine Robinson, Amy's mother.

A Simple Stone

MR. ROBINSON

We children run with glee
to sit by your knee.

A man, with boyish grin
our hearts to win.

We circle round
with giggles.

In our place we wiggle,
questions asked.

To teach
no simple task.

Young minds so fresh
New thoughts impress.

What secrets today,
hidden away.

What knowledge packed
in your brown paper sack.

Raymond F. Bergeron

We the children of the church
say, "thank you, Mr. Robinson."

For all the things you show.
For our minds to grow.

A Simple Stone

NANCY

I'm Nancy!
I'm a runner!

God gave me this gift,
My heart to uplift.

To race the wind
I run for me, and for Him.

This inner strength inside of me,
From life's stress I flee.

My self to test
Against the best.

Over this hill, my crest
To do my personal best.

My body screams
Like a nightmare dream.

The pain!
One more second to gain.

From my brain endorphins rush
My heart to thrust.

Raymond F. Bergeron

Faster, and faster I race
The time to chase.

The finish line to embrace.

I dance with the wind
Little me.

I'm Nancy!

I run free
For me and He!

A Simple Stone

They quietly quell their fears,
As twilight nears.

Old men, with glassy eyes they gaze,
And quest the clock.

And watch the second hand
Silently sweep away their lives.

Granny's Donut Shop in Long Beach, California, is the source of many of my poems. It is a kaleidoscope of races and cultures. If you are friendly and a good listener, your cup will overflow.

Raymond F. Bergeron

HERITAGE

Lee and Loy, faces of joy.
Their smiles will warm your heart.

Faces of life and death,
Faces of the martyred, murdered and massacred.

The faces of genocide,
Politically killed, their screams echo still.

Millions of souls silently scream
From their mass graves.

Their lives not saved
From their nations' nightmare dream.

The Khmer Rouge, Cambodia runs red,
With the blood of the dead.

In Pol Pot's name
The earth to flood with the blood of shame.

Faces of hunger and horror,
Faces of honor, hope and heritage.

Faces of fleeing families
And their destiny.

A Simple Stone

Lee and Loy,
Faces of the free.

Lee and Loy are Cambodian refugees who survived the Pol-Pot regime. They met and married in America. They are raising their family in Long Beach, CA where they own and operate Granny's Donut Shop.

Raymond F. Bergeron

THE DRUNKARD

The drunkard feasts his bottled stew,
And quaffs the nut-brown brew.

The barley grain that blots his brain,
And drowns the inner you.

He guzzles the grog, that garrotes his soul,
And licks the barm from his lips.

The kiss of death, the thirst he cannot quench,
He denies his opulent drunkenness.

And sees the world through opaque eyes,
And in sodden slumber dies.

The Drunkard, The Snake Pit, and Dennis Who?, are all about the same person. Dennis was an alcoholic who would sell his soul for a can of beer. He had a love-hate relationship with his father. In sodden slumber, Dennis died shortly after these three poems were written. He was fifty-four years old.

A Simple Stone

SNAKE PIT

I was a good son.
And my violent, villainous father's pride, I never won.

His viper's venomous vomit spewed,
To poison a boy he never knew.

The serpent speaks no truth,
With his forked tongue my soul he slew.

He killed my will,
And I became mentally ill.

I despair with depression,
And delusions of reality.

I struggle valiantly,
To vindicate my life and set it free.

I have visions of Valhalla,
To vanquish my father's memory.

Before he,
By my own hand, murders me.

THOU SHALL NOT KILL!
Vengeance is mine said the Lord.

Raymond F. Bergeron

I will wield the justice sword,
And I will judge the verdict throughout eternity.

A Simple Stone

DENNIS WHO?

Murdered, his self-esteem slain,
The devil's sword dripping with the blood of the barley grain.

It stains his heritage
And blots out his name.

And he disappears into nothingness,
Where only God can see.

Raymond F. Bergeron

WHY ME?

My time dwindles from the hourglass.
My dust, and dreams, that will never be.

Nigh is the reaper
And I war with God!

With anger and despair
I shake my fist at the Almighty!

I disdain His righteousness
And my wrath rattles His gates!

Will I, in Heaven's battle fall
And hear the bugle's final call?

To be cast into Satan's sea,
My soul to drift for eternity.

Or will I make peace with God
And will He heed my mortal plea?

Why me?

Why Me? is about a struggling artist/illustrator who had just made the "big-time" when he found out he had terminal cancer.

A Simple Stone

WORD WARRIOR

A warrior staunch and proud
Hidden behind a shadowed shroud.

He wears his armor well.
It shields him from his inner hell.

A fire that boils his blood
And vents with anger flood.

He wars the dragon of old,
A beast that he battled, so bold.

His weapons of words are sharp
And his barbs always find their mark.

A sneer…a scowl…a snarl,
And language howling foul!

A wounded warrior proud,
Shunned by the silent crowd.

Slashed by the sword of society
Yet, he still strides with dignity.

I look beyond his fearsome stare
To see what pain is hidden there.

Raymond F. Bergeron

The words he could not feast,
Now vanquish the dragon beast!

Written for Paul, an anti-social, ill-tempered seventy-five year old who overcame his illiteracy.

A Simple Stone

NIGHT WATCH

Nigh is the Nightingale,
And the Night Hawk wars the sun.

In horizon's tomb,
Vanquished, lies the fallen foe.

Nature's nocturnal strife,
To live one's life.

And endless battle,
Of the light, and the dark.

In darkness' veil,
In silent shadows that swallow her soul.

She dances with the moon and stars,
In the jet of heaven's sea.

Between dusk and dawn,
She sings the Whippoorwill's song.

The sun has heard her melody,
Reborn, rises to make peace with thee.

Raymond F. Bergeron

A MAN CALLED BUD

Parked by the curb,
Under the canopy of an ancient shade tree,
Rests an antiquated relic of a 1964 Ford van.

Its unkept faded paint,
Mirrors its owner, a man called Bud.
A friendly recluse, who is eight-seven years young.

All have survived the ravages of time.
A trilogy of man, machine and nature.
At peace in a world of wrath.

This is his sanctuary.
Solace for his afternoon siesta,
With his faithful dog, a rottweiler named Teddy.

They slumber, as the summer sea breeze
Scents the August air.
And, songbirds sing their lullaby.

In the van,
Adorned with a tapestry of calendars
Of bare breasted women.

A man called Bud,
Who is on the threshold of eternity.
His real name, Fred, rests his weary bones.

A Simple Stone

He reclines on his sofa of solace
In a sanctity of sleep,
He rejuvenates his mind and body.

Dreaming
Of large bosomed maidens,
That halo his head.

Raymond F. Bergeron

NEIGHBORS

Goodbye,
It's time to go.

We leave our friends and neighbors,
And part with a heavy heart.

In a fine farewell feast
We savored the wine and beast.

We have broken the bread
And it bonds our souls.

It is time that brought us
And it is time that has cast us away.

We journey to new horizons,
To vista a new day.

The die is cast.
Our time has dwindled from the glass.

Goodbye.
It's time to go.

A Simple Stone

THE CHOIR

Choirs, song of search.
New voices from the church.

This quest of soprano, alto, tenor, bass,
Your voice to grace.

Does the anthem ring
Make your heart to sing?

Does the tune
Your mind consume?

Does the melody
Your soul to free?

To praise God in harmony.
Come! Sing with me.

Raymond F. Bergeron

BRIDGE ON NEW YEAR'S EVE 1993

Its time to **deal** a new **hand**.
Will we be bold
With the **cards** we hold
Or fold and **pass?**
Our health to keep
And wealth to seek.
Will we gamble with a **finesse**
And hope for the best?
May your **trump** be long
If you guess wrong.
I **bid** you cheer
For a **grand slam** New Year.

A Simple Stone

JIMMY'S KITCHEN

When it's breakfast you seek
Come to Jimmy the Greek.

Your breakfast desire
Will soon be on his fire

He is a golden Greek god
In the kitchen he's lord.

He will cook your order in a flash
While his wife, Maria, handles the cash.

The waitresses are all southern belles
Sassy and Classy as hell!

They will serve you well
So come and sit a spell.

Like the guys at Duke Power,
Who sit by the hour.

His breakfast is great
So bring a friend or a mate.

When your hunger needs a fix
Come to Jimmy's on Sixty-Six.

Raymond F. Bergeron

ART CLASS

Raymond Reid's art class, Two Thousand and Two
He seeks the talent hidden in you.

Raymond's artist's clan,
They come with paintbrush in hand.

Seniors, bright and witty
Paint their pictures pretty.

Raymond's Rembrandt rebels rise. Hear their joyful cry.
Life has not passed them by.

They paint with bold artistic strokes
And laugh, giggle and tell off color jokes.

They've been around awhile
And each has their own special style.

They love life and are full of happiness and hope,
Because they are just plain old fashion folk.

A Simple Stone

JEANETTE

She's a southern gal
And she's my pal.

Jeanette is her name
And bridge is her game.

At the bridge table
She's quite able.

She's full of grace
But will trump your ace.

She's a card-playing dame
And I have heard her exclaim,

"I just love this game"!!!

Have a GRAND SLAM day.

Raymond F. Bergeron

ODE TO IKO

My name is Iko,
And some say I'm king of psycho.

I have no pedigree,
But I do have a few fleas.

I'm not very smart,
But I have a loving heart.

I'm an odd kind of dog,
Round like a log.

With a tail that wags,
And ears that sag.

My body's too long
And my legs are too short.

I'm a good sport,
And I can jump off the back porch.

I can run fast,
And chase a ball through the grass.

I'm not your everyday Rover.
I know no tricks, and I won't sit or roll over.

A Simple Stone

I'm very brave and bark at strangers.
And protect my master from all dangers.

I do have some fears,
Loud noises hurt my ears.

Sounds like fireworks and thunder,
The house, I will hide under.

Like any pet, I don't like the vet,
And I have some bad habits.

I lick dust from the floor
And jump on the screen door.

I don't ask for much,
A little water and food.

A pat on the head,
And a place for my bed.

I'm not a prince or a frog.
I'm just the ultimate dog.

Raymond F. Bergeron

CHARLIE

I am a white pine tree
That grew beside the windswept sea.

I came from the State of Maine
To meet my native carver, who is my surrogate father.

I have ears that sag,
And a tail that does not wag.

Eyes that do not see,
And feet that do not run.

I am BIG and BOLD
With a wooden heart and soul.

I am,
More precious than Midas gold.

I am a white pine log
Carved to be a wooden dog.

A Simple Stone

"I'LL BE OKAY"

My neighbors Jack and Jackie:
He climbed his ladder too high, "Be careful!" was her cry.

He's a spry old guy, and climbed it to the sky.
But, doesn't he know he can't fly?

"I'll prune those tree limbs" he quipped
As he let his chain saw rip!

The ladder tipped,
And he lost his grip.

Now Jack flipped,
He cracked nine ribs, a shoulder and his hip.

"I'll be okay," he said.
"Just give me a cold cloth for my head."

His wife called 911 instead!
She knew best, many years they are wed.

Now with his impish grin,
He takes his wheel chair for a spin.

"Tomorrow," he said, "is a new day."
"I'll be okay."

Raymond F. Bergeron

NANCY'S DREAM

Sleep my bar-less cage
Where the whirling twisters rage.

To dream with cryptic fright
When the spinning comes in the dead of night.

I soar beyond my earthly bonds
To witness the universe's spiral storms.

Am I a child of another world?
Where the rainbow cyclones swirl.

A Simple Stone

T – BIRD

As I walked to the Senior Center one day,
I passed a car along the way.

A car with much class,
Reclaimed from the past.

Owned by an English lass,
With a touch of flash.

Parked by the curb for all to view,
A 2003 bright yellow, T-Bird all shiny and new.

I remember this ghost from the past,
When I was young and brash and had no cash.

It set my heart afire,
My secret desire.

I sighed as I walked by,
"I bet this 'Tin Lizzy' can really fly."

Oh, my love is lost!
For I can't afford the cost.

Fifty years have passed,
I'm no longer young and brash.

No T-Bird,
And still no cash.

Raymond F. Bergeron

A Simple Stone

CHRIST

Raymond F. Bergeron

A Simple Stone

PRELUDE TO A BIRTH

O heart of hearts,
From heaven's hearth.

Your home fires kindle bright,
Across the ages sight.

We have seen your star,
A journey far, from spiral nebula.

We are
The keepers of the light.

We circle round
The victor's crown.

With jubilant celebration
And mystical expectation.

To kindle candle's spark,
No more to curse the dark.

To await the dawn,
And see the savior born.

Raymond F. Bergeron

CHRIST'S BIRTH

In the beginning,
In the time before time.

God and the light are one.
And the darkness could not put it out.

The dawn of man
Rises in the Creator's hand.

The generations begun,
The keeper of the light.

The line is long,
And the blood is strong.

Sons and daughters of Abraham,
Carpenters and kings.

Prophets' visions bring.
See the new born King!

A virgin birth,
Savior, of the earth

The light, now mortal flesh,
The Son of God, clings to mother's breast.

A Simple Stone

Emmanuel!
God is with us.

To save us from sin,
And death's dark din.

His light to shine upon the earth
To give men second birth.

Born in the desert night.
Heaven's dawn has broken.

Let it consume the darkness.
Let it light the path of peace.

Let us search the light
Not seen before.

Come!
Let us adore!

Raymond F. Bergeron

SERMON ON THE MOUNT

From the sermon on the mount
To preach and teach,
He knew.
For lame to walk
And blind to see
People like you and me,
He knew.
For whore to sin no more.
No stone they threw
He knew.
With Apostles by his side
On his triumphal ride
He knew.
In garden on bended knee
With a mortal plea
He knew.
His father's will
On this hill
He knew.
With stone rolled away
He is risen this day.
We know! We know!
From Galilee to galaxy

A Simple Stone

From flesh to spirit be.
He lived and died
For thee.

Raymond F. Bergeron

ASH WEDNESDAY

Ashes of death mark my furrowed brow.
The cross of Christ masks my mortal scowl.

Remember that thou art only dust.
When the reaper's sword is thrust.

May He come on stealthy feet
When alas we must meet.

May His sword be swift and sharp.
When He silences my beating heart.

Honor my flesh with tears of grief and sorrow.
For there will be no tomorrow.

When my soul departs this earthly sod
To rise and live with God!

A Simple Stone

PALM SUNDAY

Hosanna sing, His tribute bring.
From Bethany to Jerusalem He rides, as Apostles stride.

He guides their way this Spring day,
Men He taught to pray.

The air consumed with perfumes of desert blooms.
A journey short and sweet, palms trod beneath their feet.

Hosanna hails from this trail.
His lifelong task…His destiny…to ride this dusty path.

To Passover He rides on lowly beast.
The bitter wine of truth to feast.

With Apostles by His side,
He rides to die.

In the upper room, this last supper.
"Remember me," he spoke, as the bread He broke.

The cup they shared
But… one was not there.

Thirty pieces in his purse, forever cursed.
A Judas kiss. Betrayed!

Peter, His rock, "I know Him not!"
Denied! Rejected! Hear…the crowing of the cock.

Raymond F. Bergeron

MAUNDY THURSDAY

Hear my plea
my mortal cry.

Unseen veil
by my side.

No shadow cast
as it passes.

This unearthly presence
no human sense
can defense

This rapture
my soul to capture.

No shadow cast
as it goes.

Other souls
to behold.

A Simple Stone

GOOD FRIDAY

What wrath
This path.

To Gogoltha's Crest
This hill of death.

This mortal strife
To give one's life,

On this bloody tree
For all to see.

The Son of God, impaled
With traitor's nails.

The throng's cry
"Crucify!"

How wrong,
This gruesome song.

Crucify!
Let Him die!

Soldiers jeer
As strangers cheer.

Raymond F. Bergeron

His Father's trust
As spear they thrust.

"It is finished!" he cried,
Crucified!

A Simple Stone

ELIO

My God, My God,
Why have you forsaken me?

From death's dust
I thirst.

The bitter wine
Cannot quench.

Your cup I drink,
My destiny, fulfilled.

No more the breath
On Calvary's crest.

Fling wide the temple doors,
Heaven's hearth revealed.

Beyond the cross I reach,
My Father to embrace.

Hear His weeping,
Heaven's mournful wail.

He grieves…
For Me!

Disciple,
In delusion flee.

Raymond F. Bergeron

Oh, women of Galilee,
Care for me.

Lift gentle, from Father's yoke,
And wrap with linen cloak.

Before the Sabbath shone,
Lay my flesh on simple stone.

My body wed,
In trilogy.

I died for all,
And heed my Father's call.

A Simple Stone

CRUCIFIED

On Calvary's crest,
Stands a cross of death, hung with Heaven's flesh.

The Son of God impaled with traitor's nails,
On this bloody tree for all to see.

Born the son of Mary,
This burden, this cross I carry.

My God! My God!
Why have you forsaken me?

From death's dust I thirst,
The bitter wine cannot quench.

My Father's will on this hill,
I pray, as soldiers slay!

From my wounded side,
My blood, the earth to flood!

Beyond the cross I reach,
My Father to embrace.

Hear his weeping, heavens mournful wail,
He…grieves for me.

Raymond F. Bergeron

I heed my Father's call,
And died, to cleanse the sins of all.

CRUCIFIED!

A Simple Stone

MARY

In the shadow of the cross
She stood in silent grief.
Do they know or care
Why she's there?
With horror and disbelief,
She watches.
His life, she cannot save.
They crucify!
From the shadow of the manger
She kept, from all danger.
On this hill of wrath!
Now a stranger.
From the shadow of his light
She watched him grow.
His father's path
He chose to go.
Evermore by His side
Their shadows cast as one.
This virgin mother
and her son.

Raymond F. Bergeron

RESURRECTION

"He is not here!" Mary stands with trembling fear
Where is her son she loved so dear?

He greets the sunrise,
Rebirth, he is risen from the darkness of the tomb.

He has cast away this earthly ground,
To rise to Heaven's crown.

Heaven's blood and breath,
Has shed his mortal flesh.

On Calvary's Crest he died for you and me,
Now rises as spirit free.

Death, where now thy victory?
For he rises in Trinity.

From the grave to Heaven's throne,
He ascends to his eternal home.

"He is not here!"
For He lives in our hearts.

The stone has been rolled away,
Christ the Lord has risen today!

A Simple Stone

EASTER DAWN

From the dawn of creation
The sun has risen.
God's spirit commands
This fiery birth.
From this planet
We call Earth.
From its dust
He made us,
And gave His Son
To guide our way.
He is risen
This Easter dawn.
The light of the Earth
Has been reborn.

Raymond F. Bergeron

BETHANY

Bethany,
What draws Him there?

Is it a woman fair,
With raven hair?

His feet to cleanse
With flowing locks.

Were they just friends,
Her honor to defend
Again and again?

From Bethany
To heaven,
He did ascend.

This friendly harmony
I think He, loved she.

This woman
From Bethany!

A Simple Stone

FAITH

Raymond F. Bergeron

A Simple Stone

PRAYER

With God to commune,
A Holy quest of mortal flesh.

A silent thought.

A whispered breath.

A shout of anger and despair.

He answers all
These earthly calls.

In the power of prayer,
He's always there, His love to share.

For you, His love is vast.
Just ask!

Raymond F. Bergeron

I AM

I am Alpha and Omega
I am who I say I am

I am the light of the world
I am the one, the way and the bread of life

Whomsoever believes in Me
Shall not perish, but will have everlasting life

The pathway to Heaven's hearth
Passes through the Shepherd's gate

For I am the resurrection
And the Life

I have prepared a place
For you, and you and you!

I am the Father, the Son
And the Holy Ghost

A Simple Stone

THIRST

I've eaten the forbidden fruit
From the tree of life.

I've drunk from the well of sin.

I've tasted the bitter sweet of life.

I know the oneness of a woman.
Bonded together with love until death.

I know life's stress.

I know its anger.

I know its love.

I know the oneness of the spirit.

I have eaten His bread
And drank from His cup.

I have drunk from His well.
The living waters.

My thirst is quenched!

Raymond F. Bergeron

I'M LOVE!

Your eyes I read,
Your vacant stare,
What pain hidden there?

I've screamed your silent screams.
I've dreamed your nightmare dreams.

I'm Love!

The shame,
You're not to blame!
Your self-esteem to reclaim.

I'm Love!

May I reach inside to touch the pain,
To search its hiding place
And unmask its face?

I'm love!

By Father and Son
Raymond and Mark Bergeron

Teenage suicide is the number three cause of death for youth in America. This poem was co-written with my son Mark because I needed to see the problem through younger eyes. I wanted to offer comfort and hope to the living.

A Simple Stone

JESUS WEPT
This gift of life,
This breath.

Vanquished
My untimely death.

This mortal stress
Of earthly quest.

What wrath this path
Its shadows cast?

Life consumed,
Captured by the tomb.

Tears of grief and despair,
What sorrow carried there?

Jesus wept!
His promise kept.

His love is great,
Past through the shepherd's gate.
To pastures green,

With God to dream.
Jesus Wept. John 11:35

Raymond F. Bergeron

BUNKER HILL

In the early gray dawn
We gather to await the sunrise.

To witness a rebirth
The sun breaching from the earth.

Where fields of tobacco still grow
And, you can hear the calling of the crow.

Beside a field of polished stones
Where our ancestral spirits roam.

Who once were flesh and bone
This now their hearth and home.

Standing in the dewy grass
We embrace the shadows of the past.

Upon their timeworn graves
Their blood, our shadows cast.

We stand in God's brilliant rays
We pray and sing his praise.

Hand bells ring,
And, robins echo His name.

Beneath the eternal glow
Our faith renewed and reborn this Easter morn.

A Simple Stone

This is my first Easter after my open-heart surgery. I too have been reborn. Praise God!

Raymond F. Bergeron

CROSS WALK

Kernersville Cross Walk, Two Thousand and One.
Not by all, just some.

Christians came to march in the rain
To praise and honor our Savior slain.

To Golgotha's Crest we trod
To see our crucified Lord.

Wayside crowds stop and stare, "What are they doing there?"
The traffic their way to impair.

In somber silence we stride.
Some shuffle and even stumble.

The cross we carry so humble.
Its burden our sins and theirs to bear.

Our walk they did not share.
Maybe they don't even care!!!

A Simple Stone

PUMPKIN PATCH

Journey beyond horizon's door and reach beyond sunrise,
For you have the Lord's work to do.

God's speed your pumpkin run,
And follow the rising sun.

We pray for your safe arrival,
And your cargo's survival.

Beyond the Eastern hills,
You'll find a town called Kernersville.

Through the mountain gap,
We are more than just a dot on the map.

Hear your diesels sing,
Your treasures bring.

More precious than gold,
Hope and faith to uplift new souls.

At Bunker Hill,
We serve our Lord's will

So bring those pumpkins big and small,
We'll sell 'em all!!!

Raymond F. Bergeron

WAGON OF LIFE

The wagon of life
Full of its burdens.
You hold the reins.

What road?
What path do you choose?
Right or wrong!

Is your spirit strong
To pull its heavy load?

Or weak to fall
And be crushed by its weight?

God's path
His road is straight.

No detours,
No muddy road,
No broken bridges.

His spirit will lift you,
Lighten your burden
And light your way.

A Simple Stone

HUMANITY

Raymond F. Bergeron

A Simple Stone

911

Nine One One, Two Thousand and One
Twin towers shone in the morning sun.

They soared from their earthly home
Steel and stone reaching for heaven's throne.

Like cathedral spires
Twin Goliaths reaching higher and higher.

Twin giants guarding their city's gates
Vanquished, they stand no more.

Slain by terrorist stones
Their wrath hurling death and destruction from the azure sky.

God, hear our mournful cry
For thousands die.

No more the breath
At towers rest.

Buried in a mass communal grave
American heroes could not save.

America, hold your banner high
Less our freedoms die.

Raymond F. Bergeron

SARAJEVO

Sarajevo
Playground to battleground.

Hear your children weep,
No more the games to keep.

Now in battle fall,
And hear the bugle's final call.

They run through sniper's alley,
Ten-thousand now the tally.

How many more
To see death's valley?

Their blood,
The earth to flood.

The stain
Of ethnic cleanse!

Peace on Earth
They wonder when?

A Simple Stone

DIANA
THE SOUND OF SILENCE

The Kingdom,
Come to bury their Princess.

Their beloved "English Rose", her radiant bloom consumed,
Withered on the stem, never to grow again.

The world weeps
And millions grieve and mourn her passing.

The somber sounds of death.
Its sadness swells the summer breeze.

Slowly beats the muffled drum
And hark the bagpipes muted hum.

Her shrouded coffin on royal caisson rolls.
Hear the church bell's mournful toll.

Chestnut stallions plod,
Their hoofs clicking the cobbled sod.

Their heads bobbing with dignity,
As wayside throngs sob silently.

Her sons stride their mother's path,
The blood, the die is cast.

Raymond F. Bergeron

The Abbey's anthems ring.
As choir their tribute sing.

Friends, family and Church, echo their eulogies,
They bid a sad goodbye, and wipe a tearful eye.

The ebony hearse, showered with bouquets of flowers
Ferries her through a sea of love, to her ancestral home.

To rest on hallowed island green,
Never to be Queen, but with God to dream.

A Simple Stone

TWO WOMEN

The reaper smiles,
And weds the dead.

The bride of royalty and the bride of poverty.
A princess and a nun, become the brides of death.

The pendulum of time has swung.
Its double edge sword slaying old and young.

Millions mourn as the world weeps,
With tears of grief and despair.

Tears that nourish their ideals
And rejoice their birth.

The church bells toll,
And the silence of death…echoes the earth.

Raymond F. Bergeron

HER MAJESTY

Morning mist shrouds Mary's grace,
Her Majesty.

The sapphire sea beneath her keel,
Caresses her sculptured steel.

Her regal silhouette,
Crowns the harbor's crest.

The Queen,
The sea no more her throne.

She moors beside a quay of stone,
Her Long Beach home.

Renowned in style and sovereign speed,
In peace and war she rules the sea.

With "blood, sweat and tears",
She survived the valiant years.

Now she has laid to rest her scepter's rod,
And sheathed her heroine's sword.

The tides of time,
Have diminished her royal beauty.

A Simple Stone

Her destiny anchors beyond horizon's door
Her dignity to restore.

Her Majesty!

Saved from the scrap heap, the Queen Mary still rests regally in Long Beach, CA.

Raymond F. Bergeron

DEATH WATCH

Timothy McVeigh, his final judgement day,
Some cheer while others pray.

Like vultures they flock,
To watch the turning of the clock.

Circling on the winds of time,
Reliving his horrific crime.

To feast on the blood of the 168 souls slain,
Can you remember their names?

In the house they call death,
His final breath.

In a room of pastoral green,
7:14 his final dream.

A Simple Stone

THE LAST WARRIOR

Mankind extinct.
Too many wars I think.

I have heard the bugle's clarion call.
And in valiant battle fall.

The Earth runs red with the blood of the dead
A stain that can not be purged.

I have journeyed the path of no return.
And bravely marched into oblivion.

The grim reaper has won his ultimate prize
As the last warrior dies.

And the planet Earth spinning through space
No longer harbors the human race.

None, not even one,
Will see the tears on God's face.

Raymond F. Bergeron

A Simple Stone

EPILOGUE

Standing on the edge of eternity, the last step we take in this life will be the beginning of the next.

A Simple Stone

LAST STEPS

When Monarchs crown the milkweed
And dance with its silken seed,

When loons' lyrics swoon
And the ganders guide down the compass ring,

When Libra rules the night
And waxes the harvest moon,

It calls the hoar-frost
That paints the pumpkin's flesh and whitens the withered sod.

Beware the Autumnal chill
That warns our blood of winter's kill.

Too soon our footprints vanish on frozen ground,
And in spring will not be found.

Raymond F. Bergeron

ABOUT THE AUTHOR

Raymond is a Maine native, known to his friends and hunting buddies as "Berg". He was born and raised in the small coastal town of Kennebunk, where he graduated from the local high school. He then served his country in the military: USMCR and USAF.

Raymond and his wife Sharon have been married for forty-five years. They have three children and four grandchildren. For many years, he owned and operated a landscaping and firewood business and was a member of Rotary International.

In 1995 he moved to Long Beach, California, then to Kernersville, North Carolina in 1999, where he resides today. Raymond did not start writing poetry until he was fifty-six years old. He is also an avid bridge player and an accomplished woodcarver.

Raymond often reads his poems in local churches, senior centers, and book clubs. His heavy Maine accent adds a new dimension to his poems. Raymond's strong faith in God and love of nature are the subjects of many of his poems, which he hopes the reader enjoyed.

Raymond would enjoy hearing your comments. He can be reached at raymond@asimplestone.com